Knowing Him

Devotional Readings
for the Easter Season

ALSO BY MEL LAWRENZ

How to Understand the Bible (WordWay, 2014)

Spiritual Influence: The Hidden Power Behind Leadership (Zondervan, 2012)

Overcoming Guilt and Shame (co-authored, WordWay, 2015)

I Want to Believe: Finding Your Way in An Age of Many Faiths (Regal, 2007)

Whole Church: Leading from Fragmentation to Engagement (Jossey-Bass/Leadership Network, 2009)

Patterns: Ways to Develop a God-Filled Life (Zondervan, 2003)

Putting the Pieces Back Together: How Real Life and Real Faith Connect (Zondervan, 2005)

FOR MORE RESOURCES

www.WordWay.org

Do you ever wish you understood the Bible better?

Almost everyone does. Mature believers and new believers. Young and old. Those who have read the Bible for years and those just starting out.

How to Understand the Bible: A Simple Guide, will help you gain an overall perspective on the flow and meaning of Scripture. It addresses questions like: What is the big picture of the Bible? What about Bible translations? How should we understand the stories of the Old Testament? How should we interpret what the prophets had to say? How should we understand the teachings of Jesus? What was Jesus teaching in the parables? How can we hear God's voice in Scripture? What are the proper ways to apply Scripture to life today? Available at

KNOWING
HIM

DEVOTIONAL READINGS
FOR THE EASTER SEASON

MEL LAWRENZ

WWW.WORDWAY.ORG

WordWay

Knowing Him

Copyright © 2015 Mel Lawrenz

This title is available as a Kindle ebook.

Requests for information should be addressed to:

WordWay Resources P.O. Box 231, Waukesha, WI 53186

Published by WordWay Resources LLC

www.wordway.org

All Scripture quotations, unless otherwise indicated, are
taken from The Holy Bible, New International Version.
Copyright © 1973, 1978, 1984, 2011, by Biblica, Inc.

Cover and interior design: Sheila Hahn

CONTENTS

This symbol, the so-called "crossed cross," appears in many contexts in history. It is thought that the four crosses, recalling the death of Jesus, extend in all four directions, north, south, east, west, representing the spread of the gospel of Christ to the four corners of the Earth.

To the Reader

[The 22 readings in this book may be read at any time, but will conclude on Easter Sunday if you begin on the Sunday three weeks early, and read once piece a day. The final two chapters are essays of further reflection on salvation, the cross, and the resurrection.]

The life and teachings of Jesus are worth a lifetime of study, contemplation, and application. So too his death and resurrection. Jesus made it very clear that he had a purpose in coming, and that this purpose would be fulfilled at the time when he was betrayed, handed over to the authorities, killed, and raised from the dead.

And so for centuries in the spring of the year, around the time of the Passover, Christians have turned their attention to the accounts of the suffering of Jesus, and of his astonishing resurrection from the dead.

The apostle Paul said: ""I want to know Christ—yes, to know the power of his resurrection and participation in his sufferings, becoming like him in his death, and so, somehow, attaining to the resurrection from the dead" (Philippians 3:10-11).

In his book, *The Cruciality of the Cross*, P. T. Forsyth said: "Christ is to us just what his cross is. All that Christ was in heaven or on earth was put into what he did there . . . You do not understand Christ till you understand his cross."

Emil Brunner said: "He who understands the cross aright... understands the Bible, he understands Jesus Christ." (*The Mediator*).

And in *The Truth of God Incarnate*, Stephen Neill said "the death of Christ is the central point in history; here all the roads of the past converge; hence all the roads of the future diverge."

May these short readings give you the opportunity to reflect on the truth about what God did for the human race in Christ.

—Mel Lawrenz

www.WordWay.org

1

FREEDOM IN CHRIST

It is for freedom that Christ has set us free. Stand firm, then, and do not let yourselves be burdened again by a yoke of slavery.

— Galatians 5:1

What a bold claim!

Because Christ came, because he lived a perfect life and died a sacrificial death, because he rose from the dead on the third day, we can be free! Free from what? One can think of all the things that put the human soul in bondage. Fear of death? Yes! Jesus went there, came through on the other side, and said we could join him. Sin? Yes! God wants us to be free from the taskmaster that is sin. He wants us to be liberated from our own limitations, our obsessions, addictions, and bondage. Evil? Yes! We can be free from the power of the Evil One as we come to believe that Jesus stomped on his head (Genesis 3:15) and Satan's power can never rival God's.

The cross of Christ frees us from spiritual diversions that do not move us closer to God. It tears down temples and rituals and regimens. It nullifies self-righteousness and spiritual pride. The apostle Paul says in this verse that this message of the crucifixion of Jesus, this once-for-all antidote for our spiritual disease, is Christ's work and his grace.

So the choice is this—hang on to the notion that we are to perform well and hope God gives us a reward for a job well done, or come to the crucified Jesus, be humbled by him, and let his work set us free.

Ponder This: What is limiting your freedom today? And how might this apply to you: "It is for freedom that Christ has set us free"?

KNOWING HIM

2

WHAT MUST BE

"But what about you?" he asked. "Who do you say I am?"

Peter answered, "God's Messiah."

*Jesus strictly warned them not to tell this to anyone.
And he said, 'The Son of Man must suffer many things
and be rejected by the elders, the chief priests and the
teachers of the law, and he must be killed and on the
third day be raised to life."*

— Luke 9:20-22

It must have been a moment of extreme wonder
and bewilderment. Jesus had taken his disciples to
a remote spot to the north of Galilee, out to the
edges of Gentile territory, and there he asked them
if they understood who he was. Peter got it. Perhaps he was the first, or perhaps he was the only
one to see it. Their rabbi, whom they had left their
homes to follow, was actually the Messiah of God,
the one wrapped in prophecy and mystery. "You
are the Christ (Messiah, the Anointed One)," Peter
said.

But then, just as quickly, Jesus told them he
would be killed. It would happen not at the hand of
someone deranged and not by the Romans, but by
the spiritual leaders of the land. They would reject
him, and they would kill him. This did not add up.
Messiah was to be the great ruler, the ultimate king,

the deliverer. He was supposed to be the victor, not a victim.

At this time Peter and the rest could not see the plan of God for the ages. They had no inside information on a plan of rescue for the human race that had been arranged before the creation. They could not see millions of people in the 21st century bowing before the Lord Christ, thanking him for making them clean.

We must never second-guess God's way of salvation. We should not be surprised that God's ways exceed our comprehension. Once we see God's wisdom—as did Peter, eventually—we gain a life-changing purpose and message: "We declare God's wisdom, a mystery that has been hidden and that God destined for our glory before time began" (1 Cor. 2:7).

Ponder This: What do you think your reaction would have been if you'd been one of Jesus' followers and heard these words?

3

GREATER LOVE

"As the Father has loved me, so have I loved you. Now remain in my love. If you obey my commands, you will remain in my love, just as I have obeyed my Father's commands and remain in his love. I have told you this so that my joy may be in you and that your joy may be complete. My command is this: Love each other as I have

loved you. Greater love has no one than this: to lay down one's life for one's friends."

—John 15:9-13

Jesus said, "They hated me without reason." He was neither the first nor the last person to be subjected to senseless rejection and persecution. But because he was the only perfect, sinless one, the hatred played out against him was the vilest the world would ever see. His haters called light darkness; they saw righteousness and called it wickedness. They even called the work of God the deeds of the devil.

We've heard stories of brave sacrifices—a soldier throwing his body on a hand grenade, a bystander pulling someone off a subway track, a firefighter charging into an inferno only to lose his own life. These are stirring, and they show humanity at its best. But Jesus' sacrifice was not the impulse of a desperate moment. He moved with resolve toward his own end. There truly is no greater love. We could look through every page of history and into every corner of the universe, and we wouldn't find anything that even comes close. Jesus looked at his friends, told them he would be laying down his life, and then required one simple thing of them (and us): love each other.

And so our one real chance at loving others is if we fully receive the love of God for us and let it change our entire perspective on our relationships with others. But this won't happen by a casual remembrance of the love of Jesus. When Jesus said, "Remain in my love," he meant we are to dwell there. We are to be conscious every hour of the day that the bedrock truth of our lives—the core of our identity—is we are loved by Jesus the Christ. Keeping our focus on the cross is the way to remain in his love.

Ponder This: What do you have to say to Jesus who laid down his life for you?

4

MARKETPLACE IN THE
WORSHIP PLACE

Jesus entered the temple courts and drove out all who were buying and selling there. He overturned the tables of the money changers and the benches of those selling doves. "It is written," he said to them, "'My house will be called a house of prayer,' but you are making it a 'den of robbers.'"

— Matthew 21:12-13

To begin the last week of his life on earth (sometimes called Passion Week), Jesus entered Jerusalem with incredible drama. What must his disciples have thought? He rode down the hillside path as throngs of people shouted his praises, and he approached the beautiful temple on the other side of the valley. He then entered its courts and cleansed the temple. Sheep scattered throughout the courtyard, doves flew out of their broken cages, coins bounced and rolled across the stone plaza. And there was Jesus in the middle of it all, driving away the merchants who saw the temple courtyard as a great place to cash in.

Now Jesus had no problem with the sacrificial system. It's in the Old Testament, and the principle of sacrificial giving is part of the plan of God. But when the din of human activity drowns out the prayers of the people of God, it has gone too far.

The temple as "a house of prayer" was to be a place where the worshiper was caught up with awe for the Almighty. It was a place where people could have an encounter with their Father and Lord. The hubbub of institutionalized religiosity was a poor substitute. And so Jesus entered Jerusalem at the start of that important week, and he smashed everything that did not fit with God's character.

Sometimes God can only build after he has torn down.

Ponder This: What part of your life might Jesus want to overturn and cleanse in order for you to start over?

5

IS THERE A WAY FOR OUR SIN
TO BE TAKEN AWAY?

The next day John saw Jesus coming toward him and said, "Look, the Lamb of God, who takes away the sin of the world! This is the one I meant when I said, 'A man who comes after me has surpassed me because he was before me.' I myself did not know him, but the reason I came baptizing with water was that he might be revealed to Israel."

Then John gave this testimony: "I saw the Spirit come down from heaven as a dove and remain on him. And I myself did not know him, but the one who sent me to baptize with water told me, 'The man on whom you see the Spirit come down and remain is the one who will baptize with the Holy Spirit.' I have seen and I testify that this is God's Chosen One."

— John 1:29-34

Back at the beginning, before Jesus had even called his first disciples, there was a moment of revelation. A wild-looking prophet named John, who was baptizing people in the Jordan River and preaching about God reigning as King, encountered Jesus of Nazareth. He looked at Jesus (who was John's own cousin), and God opened John's eyes to see that this was the one he had been prophesying about.

"Look, the Lamb of God, who takes away the sin of the world!" is what John said. What he meant was: "Look! There is our salvation! There is the one whom all of the sacrifices in the Old Testament are pointing to. God has promised to take away our sin—and now that is becoming a reality!"

The dilemma all of us face is this: What can we do with all of the mistakes, the transgressions, the shortcomings, and the sins we commit? What does God make of us? Is it really possible that God is willing to forgive?

God doesn't merely forgive sinners. He "takes away" our sin. His forgiveness is so powerful, so complete, that it is appropriate to believe our sin has been "taken away." And the sign that God has really done that is that Jesus, like a sacrificial lamb, took our sin upon himself and carried it away.

Ponder This: What makes it hard for us to believe Jesus has "taken away" our sin? Is it because sometimes we hold on to it? And if so, for what reason do we do this?

6

STATUS-SEEKERS OR
SERVANT LEADERS?

He took the Twelve aside and told them what was going to happen to him. "We are going up to Jerusalem," he said, "and the Son of Man will be delivered over to the chief priests and the teachers of the law. They will condemn him to death and will hand him over to the Gen-

*tiles, who will mock him and spit on him, flog him and
kill him. Three days later he will rise."*

*Then James and John, the sons of Zebedee, came to him.
"Teacher," they said, "we want you to do for us whatever
we ask."*

"What do you want me to do for you?" he asked.

*They replied, "Let one of us sit at your right and the
other at your left in your glory."*

*When the ten heard about this, they became indignant
with James and John. Jesus called them together and
said, "You know that those who are regarded as rulers of
the Gentiles lord it over them, and their high officials
exercise authority over them. Not so with you. Instead,
whoever wants to become great among you must be your
servant, and whoever wants to be first must be slave of
all."*

— Mark 10:32-37, 41-44

In what was the worst moment for brothers James
and John, they chose the occasion of Jesus' ominous
prediction of his suffering to see if there was some-

thing in it for them. "Do for us whatever we ask,"
they said. (A remarkable request!) Can we have the
elite spots beside you?

Some questions are innocent and open-minded;
others reveal that we are completely confused.
"You don't know that you are asking," Jesus said
(v. 38). By this he meant: "Are you really that anx-
ious to be by my side when I am slaughtered?
Would you like your own crosses? Do you really
want to focus on your own status and power? Have
you missed everything I've been trying to teach
you?"

"No," Jesus told them, "if you want to be
great—really great—then you must become slaves
and servants of all."

And then Jesus made this most amazing state-
ment: "The Son of Man did not come to be served,
but to serve, and to give his life as a ransom for
many" (v. 45). He was the fulfillment of the "suffering servant" whom the prophet Isaiah had spoken
of seven centuries earlier. (Isaiah 52:13–53:1-12)
And he was the "ransom" (Isaiah 53:10-11), the one
who would liberate us from the taskmasters of sin,
death, and the Evil One.

Ponder This: What are the biggest barriers we face in giving up our status and security, and instead living lives of servanthood?

7

BETTER THAN SILVER OR GOLD

Concerning this salvation, the prophets, who spoke of the grace that was to come to you, searched intently and with the greatest care, trying to find out the time and circumstances to which the Spirit of Christ in them was pointing when he predicted the sufferings of the Messiah and the glories that would follow....Even angels long to look into these things....

For you know that it was not with perishable things
such as silver or gold that you were redeemed from the
empty way of life handed down to you from your ances-
tors, but with the precious blood of Christ, a lamb with-
out blemish or defect. He was chosen before the creation
of the world, but was revealed in these last times for your
sake. Through him you believe in God, who raised him
from the dead and glorified him, and so your faith and
hope are in God.

— 1 Peter 1:10-23

Years after Jesus' death and resurrection, Peter
wrote about the mystery of Christ, things that
"even angels long to look into." These highest and
best truths about God include the mighty act of redemption. Jesus said he came to give his life as a
ransom (Mk. 10:45). And here Peter says we were
redeemed not by silver or gold (the richest of the
world's riches), but by "the precious blood of
Christ" (the richest of God's treasures, the life of
the very Son of God).

Redemption or ransom is at the heart of the Old
Testament pictures of salvation. It means to liberate
someone by buying them back. God asked the He-

brews to make a sacrifice of every firstborn. For sheep, goats, and the like, this meant death; but God told the Hebrews to substitute a lamb for their firstborn children. This liberation was a ransom. A lamb instead of a son. But in the case of Jesus, it was the Son instead of us.

It is difficult for us, as a practical matter, to give up the idea that money (silver and gold) is not where power really lies. We say there are some things money can't buy, and that is true when it comes to love, truth, and character. It is even truer in our relationship with God. Our power, status, and wealth do not get us one step closer to God. All of that perishes, but not "the precious blood of Christ."

Ponder This: What is something you know about Christ today that the angels would sing about?

8

ONLY GOD COULD

[Christ] is before all things, and in him all things hold together. And he is the head of the body, the church; he is the beginning and the firstborn from among the dead, so that in everything he might have the supremacy. For God was pleased to have all his fullness dwell in him, and through him to reconcile to himself all things,

*whether things on earth or things in heaven, by making
peace through his blood, shed on the cross.*

*Once you were alienated from God and were enemies in
your minds because of your evil behavior. But now he
has reconciled you by Christ's physical body through
death to present you holy in his sight, without blemish
and free from accusation—if you continue in your faith,
established and firm, and do not move from the hope held
out in the gospel.*

— Colossians 1:17-23

Anselm, writing in the 11th century, raised a
question: Why did God become man? This is the
enigma of Christ. His answer went like this: Only
man should solve the problem of sin (because sin
is, after all, a mess that human beings have made),
but only God could. A prophet dying on a cross
would at most be a martyr and a model. But Jesus
Christ was really human and also divine. Therefore, his sacrifice had a human face on it, but it is a
divine offering.

That is why a passage like Colossians 1 is so
important. It speaks of both the person of Christ,
and his work on our behalf. Regarding his person,

"he is the image of the invisible God" (v. 15), and "in him all things were created" (v. 16), and "all [God's] fullness" dwelt in Jesus (v. 19).

And so, because of who Jesus was, he was able to reconcile to God all things "by making peace through his blood, shed on the cross" (v. 20).

On that most violent of all days in human history, God was reaching out to those who were alienated from him and at enmity with him. He offered us reconciliation so we could end up "holy in his sight, without blemish and free from accusation." Only God could do that.

Ponder This: What is something about yourself that you know only God could change?

9

THE HIGHEST PRIEST

How much more, then, will the blood of Christ, who through the eternal Spirit offered himself unblemished to God, cleanse our consciences from acts that lead to death, so that we may serve the living God! For this reason Christ is the mediator of a new covenant, that those who are called may receive the promised eternal inheri-

tance—now that he has died as a ransom to set them free from the sins committed under the first covenant....

Day after day every priest stands and performs his religious duties; again and again he offers the same sacrifices, which can never take away sins. But when this priest had offered for all time one sacrifice for sins, he sat down at the right hand of God, and since that time he waits for his enemies to be made his footstool. For by one sacrifice he has made perfect forever those who are being made holy.

— Hebrews 9:14-15; 10:11-14

For centuries the Hebrew people watched their priests perform the rituals of the tabernacle and then the temple. The word priest means "one who stands," and these were indeed men who stood before God on behalf of the people, helping them bring their sacrifices in worship. And the high priest did such special things as going into the most holy place of the temple and offering the most intimate prayers on behalf of the people.

With Jesus, all of that changed. He came and took the role of the highest priest, the "one mediator between God and mankind" (1 Tim. 2:5). He came and told us that the lessons learned from the temple and the priests and the animal sacrifices—lessons about our sin and the terrible judgment pronounced on sin and the possibility of substitute sacrifices—had been learned, and he had come to be the fulfillment.

Jesus is the great High Priest. He's also the sacrifice. He came to be "the mediator of a new covenant" (Heb. 9:15). He is the ransom (redemption).

But Jesus is quite different from all of the earlier high priests. "Day after day every priest stands and performs his religious duties," but these sacrifices "can never take away sins." What those priests did was provide a picture of and a teaching about forgiveness. Jesus actually accomplished it. He was both God and man, and thus he stood before us linking heaven and earth. His death was the ultimate sacrifice, and indeed it is the only sacrifice that truly matters.

Risen from the dead and returned to the Father, Jesus continues to be the link between God and people. He doesn't "stand" anymore, however; now he sits on the throne of God.

Ponder This: What is the uppermost concern in your life today that you would like the great High Priest to bring to the throne of God?

10

RECONCILED!

For Christ's love compels us, because we are convinced that one died for all, and therefore all died. And he died for all, that those who live should no longer live for themselves but for him who died for them and was raised again....

Therefore, if anyone is in Christ, the new creation has come: The old has gone, the new is here! All this is from God, who reconciled us to himself through Christ and gave us the ministry of reconciliation: that God was reconciling the world to himself in Christ, not counting people's sins against them. And he has committed to us the message of reconciliation.

— 2 Corinthians 5:14-19

Many theologians have thought that reconciliation may be as important a word as any other in the biblical vocabulary of salvation. It is a word from the world of human relationships. It is that wonderful thing that sometimes happens when people at enmity with each other steer a course toward each other to confess wrongdoing, to repair a rift, to make up, to set aside differences, to cease hostilities, to reconcile.

Most people don't really believe they are at enmity with God. They think God is quite favorably disposed toward them. After all, why wouldn't God be? Aren't we quite lovable the way we are?

God's love is not infatuation or God just being "nice." The God of love loves the unlovable with a rigorous commitment. He loves human beings who have ignored him, who have arrogantly thought they don't really need him, and who have been gods to themselves. God's love sees us for who we can be, not who we are.

Christ, who had no sin, stood in the place of the sinner so the sinner could stand before God—enmity gone, opposition put aside, friends again.

And thus we bear a message of reconciliation, and we have a ministry of reconciliation. In other words, when people in the world think of Christians, they ought to think: *Oh yes, those are the people who are passionate about peace and reconciliation. They live in it and they live for it.*

Ponder This: Is that what people really see in our attitudes and values?

11

WHEN HE IS LIFTED UP

"Now my soul is troubled, and what shall I say? 'Father, save me from this hour'? No, it was for this very reason I came to this hour. Father, glorify your name!"

Then a voice came from heaven, "I have glorified it, and will glorify it again." The crowd that was there and

*heard it said it had thundered; others said an angel had
spoken to him.*

*Jesus said, "This voice was for your benefit, not mine.
Now is the time for judgment on this world; now the
prince of this world will be driven out. And I, when I am
lifted up from the earth, will draw all people to myself."
He said this to show the kind of death he was going to
die.*

— John 12:27-33

In that last week of Jesus' life on earth, one day he
taught about an event of the cosmos that was about
to happen. The day of his death would not just be a
martyrdom, but "the time for judgment." By a great
divine act, the Evil One himself would be driven
out, and by being "lifted up from the earth," Jesus
would draw people to himself. The crowds did
gather to watch Jesus on the cross, and since then
hundreds of millions of people have been drawn to
him as well.

Jesus said that sometimes death results in new
life. Like a seed buried in the soil, soon to erupt
into life, so would his demise be the brief prelude
before eternal life would burst upon the human

scene. It would be like that dark moment in a theater when all the lights go dim and the voices hush right before the curtain goes up, spotlights bathe the stage, and we see what the playwright really has in mind.

This would not be easy—Jesus knew that. Showing his real humanity, Jesus told his disciples that his heart was troubled. But he also told the Father: "Glorify your name!"

That's all that was needed. Soon, the disciples would be sharing their last supper with Jesus. In the meantime, they had a little while to think about seeds in the ground.

Ponder This: How would you like God to be glorified in your life?

12

SON OF DAVID, LORD OF DAVID

Then Jesus said to them, "Why is it said that the Messiah is the son of David? David himself declares in the Book of Psalms:

"'The Lord said to my Lord:
"Sit at my right hand

until I make your enemies
a footstool for your feet.'"

David calls him 'Lord.' How then can he be his son?"
— Luke 20:41-44

Jesus had many ways of saying seemingly outrageous things about himself. He said he was the Lord of the Sabbath, so he could decide what he would or would not do on the Sabbath. He let people bow down at his feet and worship him. He forgave people their sins. He let them use names for him that were reserved for God. One must conclude he was either a completely deluded person or a charlatan. Or he really was who he claimed to be. There are no other alternatives.

He was and is the Lord of King David, and, more than that, Lord of heaven and earth. This idea completely turned every expectation of Messiah upside down. People were looking for David's successor; they were not expecting David's Lord.

Jesus humbled himself and took a lowly spot, even though he is Lord of all. This is the paradox of Jesus. He will wash feet but he commands obedience. He forgives but also confronts. He assumed the shame of crucifixion but rose again in glory. This is a different kind of lordship than we'd ever expect from anyone possessing power and authority.

Ponder This: If Jesus is King of kings and Lord of lords, how does that make you look at the world differently?

KNOWING HIM

13

THE TEMPLE TOUR

Some of his disciples were remarking about how the temple was adorned with beautiful stones and with gifts dedicated to God. But Jesus said, "As for what you see here, the time will come when not one stone will be left on another; every one of them will be thrown down."

— Luke 21:5-6

The temple loomed larger than anything else in the spiritual vision of Jesus' followers. It was, after all, the embodiment of God's promise and the symbol of his presence. It was the arena for the ritual and the exercise of the law. Enthused worshipers made their pilgrimages there to make sacrifices and admire the massive, beautiful stones that made up its walls. Jesus burst the bubble of the disciples' admiration when he looked up at the impressive structure—this symbol of stability for the people—and said, "This will all be torn down one day." Shocking. Unthinkable. Subversive even. At least, that is what his enemies made of it.

It is true, of course, that all monuments made with hands and all empires built by intellect and guts do eventually crumble. It is as certain as anything in history. The temple had been destroyed before and rebuilt. But now Jesus expands his disciples' understanding by telling them of a cataclysm ahead that will tear apart families and bring war across the land. Bible interpreters' beliefs vary regarding whether this is a prophecy about the destruction of Jerusalem at the hands of the Romans some 40 years later, or a prophecy yet to be fulfilled—or both.

In either case, Jesus' principle is the same: Don't trust in what you can put your hands on. Our salvation, our redemption, is only to be found in God and his love. Indeed, Jesus said, when life seems to be falling apart around you, you should "lift up your heads, because your redemption is drawing near" (Luke 21:28). He should know. Jesus said that when the temple, which was his body, was destroyed, it would be raised in three days. And it was. Any human can rebuild stones, but only God can come back from death.

Ponder This: Are there any "temples" or sanctuaries in your life that you know could pass away, necessitating a new level of faith?

14

BOASTING ABOUT THE CROSS

Those who want to impress people by means of the flesh are trying to compel you to be circumcised.... May I never boast except in the cross of our Lord Jesus Christ, through which the world has been crucified to me, and I to the world. Neither circumcision nor uncircumcision means anything; what counts is the new creation.

— Galatians 6:12-15

Paul wrote this letter, which we call the book of
Galatians, to certain Christians who had begun
their new spiritual life with faith in Jesus, but then
were told by others that Paul's message of grace
was horribly incomplete and probably dangerous.
They taught that it is not enough to believe in Jesus
and follow him; you must also continue to observe
those hundreds of regulations in the Old Testament. Even if you are a Gentile, you should still
observe the dietary laws, the sacrifices, and circumcision, they said.

Paul saw this as a spiritual emergency, and he
wrote this letter to warn these believers not to be
bewitched by those legalists.

There is one way to God. Let the things in your
life that should die, die. Let strivings die, let legal-
ism die, let love for the world die, let personal
spiritual pride die. Resign it all, give it all over, let it
be crucified as Jesus let himself be crucified, and
you will be free.

Then we will have something to boast about.
We will brag about Jesus Christ. We will shout his
name to the world. We'll fill up with a pride not in

ourselves, but in him. And we will look at his cross and see it as a moment of glory, not shame.

Ponder This: Are there things you have been boasting about in your life? What needs to happen for you to boast only about Christ?

KNOWING HIM

15

JUSTIFIED!

All have sinned and fall short of the glory of God, and all are justified freely by his grace through the redemption that came by Christ Jesus. God presented Christ as a sacrifice of atonement, through the shedding of his blood—to be received by faith. He did this to demonstrate his righteousness, because in his forbearance he had left the sins committed beforehand unpunished—he did it to demonstrate his righteousness at the present time, so as to be just and the one who justifies those who have faith in Jesus. Where, then, is boasting? It is excluded.

— Romans 3:23-27

It is hard to overestimate the power of this one word: justified. Over the past 20 centuries, Christians have periodically rediscovered this important truth. We keep forgetting it because we are so inclined to think we can earn God's favor if we just try hard enough. But, like the love of a good parent, God's grace is something we can never earn. God gladly gives it.

Justification is a word from the law courts. What it means in the New Testament is that God, who is both Father and Judge, has said we can be acquitted at court because of the sacrifice of Jesus.

Have you seen a defendant in a courtroom receive a verdict of not guilty and walk out of the courtroom entirely free? It's decisive because it's a decision made by an authority about a change of status.

This passage teaches that because of Jesus, we can be acquitted in the court of God's law (even though we are guilty of breaking it), and walk out as free people. We are guilty (3:23). Yet Jesus voluntarily took the penalty of the world's sins on his shoulders. There is justice in it all, and God offers justification to people who ought to be penalized (3:26).

Ponder This: Having walked out of the courtroom of God's justice as a free person, what do you have to say to God?

16

THE BEGINNING BEFORE THE BEGINNING

In the beginning was the Word, and the Word was with God, and the Word was God. He was with God in the beginning…. The Word became flesh and made his dwelling among us. We have seen his glory, the glory of the one and only Son, who came from the Father, full of grace and truth.

— John 1:1-2, 14

Oftentimes we understand the beginning of a
story when we approach its end. Like the book of
Genesis, the opening words of the gospel of John
are "In the beginning." Except this beginning
stretches beyond the creation, back to a time when
there was God—and only God. There must have
been such a time, of course, because if God is the
Creator, then there was a time when it was only
God.

The great truth of Christianity here described
by John in his gospel, and repeated throughout the
New Testament, is that Jesus Christ was there before the beginning. He is the Word of God, he was
with God, and he was God. He took part in the act
of creation; he is the source of life and light.

Then one day he took human form ("the Word
became flesh"). He came to earth and lived a life
that looked just like ours, with hunger, tiredness,
and temptation—but without sin. He is the great
enigma of the history of the world. People have
worshipped him and they have hated him. They
have also tried to ignore him, but that is the least
sensible thing to do.

He is the Lord of glory. "We have seen his glory, the glory of the one and only Son, who came from the Father, full of grace and truth" (v. 14).

Ponder This: In what ways do you need the truth and grace of God through Christ at this point in your life?

17

FOOT WASHING

It was just before the Passover Feast. Jesus knew that the time had come for him to leave this world and go to the Father. Having loved his own who were in the world, he loved them to the end. The evening meal was in progress, and the devil had already prompted Judas, the son of Simon Iscariot, to betray Jesus. Jesus knew that the Father had put all things under his power, and that he had come

*from God and was returning to God; so he got up from
the meal, took off his outer clothing, and wrapped a towel
around his waist. After that, he poured water into a basin and began to wash his disciples' feet, drying them
with the towel that was wrapped around him.*

— John 13:1-5

T he final drama was drawing near. The disciples
went to the upper room where they would have the
Passover meal and Jesus would teach them about
things to come. Jesus "knew that the hour had
come." He knew "the Father had put all things under his power" and he was returning to God. And
Satan had already entered the heart of the betrayer,
Judas Iscariot.

With the stage thus set, Jesus chose to do a most
peculiar thing. He removed his outer garment,
wrapped a towel around his waist, poured water
into a basin, and began washing his disciples' feet.
Foot washing was not unusual in that world of
dusty paths and dry air. What was unusual was for
the master to do this for all of his followers and at
this moment when everything held in the balance.

"Do you understand what I have done for
you?" Jesus asked (v.12). "I am Lord. I am Master.

Yet if I serve you in this way, surely you can serve each other. And if you do, you will be blessed."

Love each other. Care for each other. Serve each other. Do the dirty work for each other. Humble yourselves before each other. Expend yourselves for each other.

One more time Jesus showed the disciples what it means to be a disciple. And he also knew that only on the other side of the cross, when they would see just how far Jesus' service would go, would they understand it all.

Ponder This: What would your reaction be if Jesus approached you to wash your feet?

18

ANOTHER COUNSELOR

"If you love me, keep my commands. And I will ask the Father, and he will give you another advocate to help you and be with you forever—the Spirit of truth. The world cannot accept him, because it neither sees him nor knows him. But you know him, for he lives with you and will be in you...."

"All this I have spoken while still with you. But the Advocate, the Holy Spirit, whom the Father will send in my name, will teach you all things and will remind you of everything I have said to you. Peace I leave with you; my peace I give you. I do not give to you as the world gives. Do not let your hearts be troubled and do not be afraid.
— John 14:15-17, 25-27

There must have been sorrow, anxiety, and hope in the air as Jesus talked with his disciples about his upcoming departure. This Upper Room Discourse in the gospel of John (chapters 13–17) was Jesus' final word to his disciples on the night he was betrayed.

In it, he spoke about "another advocate" who would come to them. This is a word that means counselor, comforter, one who comes alongside. Thinking of God the Holy Spirit as our advocate is indeed one of the most comforting thoughts a human being could have. Who else would you want with you when you go through life's victories and struggles? Who else could work in the innermost recesses of our thoughts and feelings, helping us make good choices and have a proper disposition, and giving us confidence when we need it?

When Jesus said "another advocate," he was
also teaching his disciples that what he was doing
among them and for them was to be that kind of
advocate. He had filled them with truth and hope,
with a vision of who God is and a humbling con-
cept of who they were. Now he would leave
them—a sorrowful prospect. But in all of these
ways, God would still be with them.

None of us were in that upper room; yet if Jesus
stood among us today, he would give us the same
assurance.

*Ponder This: What kind of counsel or comfort or advo-
cacy do you need from God at this time in your life?*

19

MAUNDY THURSDAY

Jesus said, "Now is the Son of Man glorified and God is glorified in him. If God is glorified in him, God will glorify the Son in himself, and will glorify him at once. My children, I will be with you only a little longer. You will look for me, and just as I told the Jews, so I tell you now: Where I am going, you cannot come. A new command I give you: Love one another. As I have loved you, so you

*must love one another. By this everyone will know that
you are my disciples, if you love one another."*

— John 13:31-35

The word *Maundy* comes from the Latin word for
commandment (*mandatum*), which Jesus talked
about when he told his disciples he was leaving
them a new command that they "love one another."

There were probably many things going on in
the disciples' minds during the Last Supper in that
upper room—including fear and bewilderment after Jesus told them someone in that very room
would betray him.

Jesus handed the betrayer a piece of bread, just
as he had been feeding all of his disciples all along.
Always giving, always gracing. Jesus fed thou-
sands of people with fish and loaves, and every
word that came out of his mouth was spiritual food
for those who listened and understood. But on this
night, he fed them differently. Passing the bread
and then the wine, he spoke ominous, comforting
words: "This is my body... This is my blood..."
This wasn't an ordinary supper—not even an ordinary Passover. His words connected with what
he'd said on the shores of faraway Galilee: "I am

the bread of life. Whoever comes to me will never go hungry, and whoever believes in me will never be thirsty.... Whoever eats my flesh and drinks my blood has eternal life, and I will raise them up at the last day" (Jn. 6:35, 54).

Jesus told them to repeat this unique meal in the future. And then it was time for them to go out into the chilly night. In a quiet garden among the olive trees, quiet but for the deep night sounds of dogs barking in the distance, Jesus prayed. In agony he prayed. The specter of shameful execution and of bearing the curse of sin tore into the human consciousness of Jesus. And in the end, it was sheer obedience to the divine plan that carried Jesus into the hands of the conspirators who were waiting for him. Did the disciples remember "the new command"?

Ponder This: What would have been going through your mind had you been one of the disciples at the Last Supper or out in the garden of Gethsemane?

20

THE CRUCIFIXION

They came to a place called Golgotha (which means "the place of the skull"). There they offered Jesus wine to drink, mixed with gall; but after tasting it, he refused to drink it. When they had crucified him, they divided up his clothes by casting lots. And sitting down, they kept watch over him there. Above his head they placed the

written charge against him: THIS IS JESUS, THE
KING OF THE JEWS.

— Matthew 27:33-37

Now came the time for the clash between good and evil, heaven and hell. The crucifixion of Jesus is both the most horrific moment in human history, and humanity's only hope. That's why we call the Friday before Easter, Good Friday.

Jesus' followers were still too weak to understand, and so they scattered. The religious elite carried out their plot. The political leaders passed the buck, and in the end, they discarded Jesus for the sake of convenience. The crowds gawked. Two thieves hung on either side of a man whose crime was hard to comprehend. The placard above his head announced with biting sarcasm: King of the Jews. That must have attracted some attention

We know of seven things Jesus said from that cross, including a pronouncement of forgiveness for the soldiers, provision for the care of his mother, and a plea for something to wet his parched mouth. But the last words on that last day of his natural human life were the most important: "It is finished!" (John 19:30).

That was not a cry of resignation, nor capitulation or surrender. It was a shout of victory that all that God had planned for the restoration of sinful human beings was now accomplished. Now there could be justification! Redemption! Reconciliation! All that needed to be done for the debt and scar of sin had been done. Forgiveness was now free.

All that remained was for Jesus to step out from the shadow of death, which he would easily do after a few days. But first, the disciples had time to search their hearts for how something good could be found in something so bad. And the enemies of God disappeared into the darkness of their own duplicity.

Ponder This: How does the crucifixion of Jesus most powerfully impact you?

21

WAITING FOR GOD

Later, Joseph of Arimathea asked Pilate for the body of Jesus. Now Joseph was a disciple of Jesus, but secretly because he feared the Jewish leaders. With Pilate's permission, he came and took the body away. He was accompanied by Nicodemus, the man who earlier had visited Jesus at night. Nicodemus brought a mixture of myrrh and aloes, about seventy-five pounds. Taking Je-

sus' body, the two of them wrapped it, with the spices, in strips of linen. This was in accordance with Jewish burial customs. At the place where Jesus was crucified, there was a garden, and in the garden a new tomb, in which no one had ever been laid. Because it was the Jewish day of Preparation and since the tomb was nearby, they laid Jesus there.

— John 19:38-42

A small act of mercy on the part of Joseph of Arimathea meant that Jesus' limp and lifeless body would not be thrown into a pit of a grave, but laid carefully in a rock-hewn garden tomb. Joseph was probably a man with significant conflicts. Wealthy and a prominent member of the Jewish council, he represented the very establishment that was committed to Jesus' demise. Yet he believed in Jesus, secretly. To believe in Jesus does put one on the spot. Being a committed disciple of Jesus always upsets the status quo.

Nicodemus, also fearful but compelled, came to the tomb as well. So two men with associations that put them at odds with Jesus, but who really wanted to believe, are the ones who respectfully wrap the body in cloths and 75 pounds of spices. Yet the only thing that can really take away the stench of death and its empty stare is resurrection.

These two men and the other disciples were still stuck in that no man's land between life and death. All Jesus' followers had to hold on to were Jesus' vague words about rising from death. Could such words be taken seriously? What would they do during these days of waiting? Would they be arrested? And so they waited behind locked doors because there was nothing else to do.

Ponder This: Is there some way in which you are waiting to see what will happen next? How will you find faith in the waiting place?

22

RESURRECTION DAY

Early on the first day of the week, while it was still dark,
Mary Magdalene went to the tomb and saw that the
stone had been removed from the entrance. So she came
running to Simon Peter and the other disciple, the one
Jesus loved, and said, "They have taken the Lord out of
the tomb, and we don't know where they have put him!"
— John 20:1-2

How difficult was it for the One who is Lord of the universe—who had a hand in creation itself, who is the very force of life that holds living things together—to wake up from the sleep of death and set aside the burial cloths draping his body?

As was always the case, Jesus' revelations of himself did not happen with television cameras focused on him. Not even a respectable crowd was gathered. An alarming word from young Mary Magdalene about Jesus' body being gone produced a panic and a footrace among two of Jesus' beloved disciples, Peter and John. One looked and merely saw the emptiness of the tomb; the other saw the connection between this moment and the mysterious words of Jesus—and he believed.

Now things were really complicated and the disciples went home. So Jesus first appeared to a brokenhearted Mary who stayed at the tomb. Mary was the first to behold something the world had never seen before—a resurrected, transformed life.

Resurrection day for Jesus was simply the first installment of a resurrection of masses of people when this era of the history of the universe draws to a close. What God promises to those who belong to Jesus is not the loss of self into a nothingness bliss, but the resurrection and remaking of every-thing that is right and good in the world he created. And until then, he invites us to begin living trans-formed lives, continually shaped and changed by the hope of the redemption of all that God has made.

Ponder This: Where in your life do you need the resur-rection power of Jesus at work today?

ESSAY

RESCUE

Excerpt (chapter 12) from *Putting the Pieces Back Together: How Real Life and Real Faith Connect* by Mel Lawrenz (Zondervan, 2005)

"I think nothing has surprised us more than to learn so many ships were near enough to rescue us in a few hours."

— *Titanic lifeboat survivor*

Surely she would escape from her kidnappers if she had the slightest chance, everyone assumed. If there was any opportunity for her to call out to someone for help, or pass a note that said, "I'm Elizabeth Smart, help me," she would. And so, for the nine months of her captivity since she was snatched from her bedroom in the middle of the night, most people assumed the worst-she must be dead.

Yet fourteen-year-old Elizabeth was very much alive. During her captivity she had been around many people, yet had not signaled for help. She was left alone at times, capable of walking away. When police approached her on the street, inquiring whether she was Elizabeth Smart, she denied it. This poor young girl, practically brainwashed by her domineering abductors, needed so much to be saved, but didn't see it, and couldn't take advantage of it. It was a good thing a police officer who recognized her on the street knew better, and was determined to find the truth.

Then there is the case of Jessica Lynch, the nineteen-year-old private, first-class, who served as part of a maintenance unit in Iraq, and who was taken captive after her convoy took a wrong turn in the city of Nasiriyah. Held for eight days in a hospital, she cried out to go home. But she could not save herself. Even without armed guards, how do you run when you have two broken legs? A few days later rescuers swooped down by helicopter, stormed the building, snatched her from her bed, and carried her to safety.

Saved From What?

Today some people think it's a joke when they hear, you must be saved. "That's the kind of thing religious kooks say," they think. "Isn't salvation an antique idea, or maybe just the mental crutch of some people who still aren't willing to stand on their own two feet, spiritually speaking? Isn't it just derelicts who need to 'come to Jesus'?"

But what if you do have two broken legs? What if we have no idea just how much trouble we are in and how desperately we need to be saved?

Almost all religions begin with the assumption that we need to be saved from that something dreadfully wrong in the world-or with us. Salvation is a belief and a hope that there is a way out of captivity, a rescue whether we need we know it or not.

Christian faith says specifically that we need to be saved from evil, from judgment, and from our own self-destructive sin. Salvation from evil means that we can hope in God's power to prevent the whole human race from descending into the deepest darkness-even though evil will keep on appearing in tomorrow's headlines until God comes to remake the world. Salvation from judgment means that, by God's gracious act of free forgiveness, he acquits us from the spiritual crimes and misdemeanors we have committed. And salvation from sin means that God's power is available to reshape our character so that we need not repeat the same mistakes over and over again.

That is precisely why the Bible speaks of salvation as a past, present, and future reality. The biblical authors say, we have been saved, we are being saved, and we will be saved.

Looking backward, the truth is that "it is by grace you have been saved, through faith-and this is not from yourselves, it is the gift of God-not by works, so that no one can boast" (Ephesians 2:8-9).

"Have been saved."

God has won the war, though the battles continue. He has sent his grace, his unstoppable intent
to pour out mercy and kindness, to the human race
like food flowing into famine and water into
parched mouths. When Jesus died on the cross, the
clash between the political powers of earth and the
dark power of the demonic and the brilliant power
of God came to a decisive climax. The light went
out for three hours, the body of the author of life
slumped against the rough wood. Perhaps Satan
laughed, then cowered. The curtain of the temple
was torn open as a sign, as if this High Priest had
stepped up to the Holy of Holies, the presence of
God, and ripped open an entryway that would forever make a relationship with God only as far away
as the words "I believe. I do believe."

But God is also continuing to save us. The battles still rage on, though the outcome is certain.
Writing from prison, the apostle Paul said, "Continue to work out your salvation with fear and
trembling," and then, to make sure that people with
broken legs didn't try to run too soon, added, "for it
is God who works in you to will and to act according to his good purpose" (Phil. 2:12-13; italics
mine). He also wrote, "The message of the cross if

foolishness to those who are perishing, but to us who are being saved it is the power of God" (1 Cor.1:18; italics mine). The process of salvation is God's faithful, constant work of educating us and shaping us and cleansing us: "I will save you from all your uncleanness" (Ezek.36:29). That means that the wisest person is the one who says, "I am unclean, I can't get the dirt off, I can't heal myself. God, please do what only you can."

Then there is future salvation. God will save us. Ask yourself, just for a moment, what you really believe is going to happen as history unfolds in ever-greater extremes.

Charles Dickens' famous opening passage from A Tale of Two Cities begins this way: "It was the best of times, it was the worst of times, it was the age of wisdom, it was the age of foolishness, it was the epoch of belief, it was the epoch of incredulity, it was the season of light, it was the season of darkness, it was the spring of hope, it was the winter of despair, we had everything before us, we had nothing before us, we were all going direct to Heaven, we were all going direct the other way."

Doesn't the world today look like just such a set of contradictions? But it's more severe than that.

The pendulum is swinging in an ever-wider arch: the best is getting better, and the worst is getting worse. History still moves toward a clash. The question of destiny should press itself on every person's mind. Some take comfort in the roll of the dice: chances are I will be able to duck the clash. But whether any of us are firsthand witnesses of the climax of history, we will all face the last door-way when we come to the end of our own lives. We all need the God who says, "In the day of salvation, I will help you" (Isa.49:8). We all need to heed the advice that "the hour has come for you to wake from your slumber, because our salvation is nearer now than when we first believed" (Rom.13:11).

The biblical word "salvation" means rescue. It means someone bigger and better, stronger and wiser, does for us what we cannot do for ourselves. The necessity of salvation takes nothing away from human dignity. Rather, it gives us back our own lives. Whether we realize we need rescue or not, we still need rescue. It just makes sense for us to admit it, and to live in such a way that we respond to the rescue.

A young woman named Mary two thousand years ago had the wisdom to know that she needed

God's salvation. She wasn't a captive to any abductor, but she knew that she was trapped by her own limitations, and as vulnerable as anyone else to a wicked neighbor, or a political regime, or falling from a building. Her song celebrated God's mighty ways of rescuing:

"My soul glorifies the Lord and my spirit rejoices in God my Savior... his mercy extends to those who fear him from generation to generation. He has performed mighty deeds with his arm" (Luke 1:46-50).

Mary's song was her response to the most incredible claim, given to her by an angel: "You will be with child and give birth to a son, and you are to give him the name Jesus."

Jesus in English, Yeshua in Hebrew, a name that simply means "Salvation." As Joseph heard from an angel in a dream, "She will give birth to a son, and you are to give him the name Jesus, because he will save his people from their sins."

There are two sides of salvation: the objective and the subjective. The first is the fact of salvation. By Jesus' coming, and by his sacrificial death and resurrection to new life, an unalterable act of salvation has occurred. The Bible has a whole vocabu-

lary to explain it: redemption, reconciliation, justification, adoption.

"Redemption," from the world of the market-
place, says that through the sacrificial death of
Christ we have been bought out of our slavery to
sin. Like slaves who are purchased in order to be
set free, God supplied the price and received the
price. All of this was depicted again and again in
the sacrificial rituals of the Old Testament. This is
true freedom, but a freedom that comes from being
owned by God: "you are not your own. You were
bought at a price. Therefore, honor God with your
body." (1 Corinthians 6:19-20).

"Reconciliation" comes from the world of relationships. The shattering effects of sin in the world
led to estrangement. We are separated from each
other, and separated from God. But in Christ, and
in his sacrifice, God provides a bridge. By faith we
are on God's side, and God calls us his friends.

"Adoption," from the realm of the family, means
that we become, through the sacrifice of Christ, true
children of God. All human beings are creations of
God, and are thus his offspring. But being a true
child is a reality of a different magnitude. It means
being an heir, and living now in conscious submis-

sion to the master of the household, the benevolent
Father. The prodigal son became a son again when
he turned back home.

"Justification" is from the world of law courts.
"Justification" and "righteousness" are in the same
word group in the New Testament. To be justified
means to be made right with God. It is what happened to Abraham when he believed God's as-
tounding promise. Justification by grace through
faith is a foundation of certainty. As Paul put it: "If
God is for us, who can be against us? He who did
not spare his own Son, but gave him up for us all-
how will he not also, along with him, graciously
give us all things? Who will bring any charge
against those whom God has chosen? It is God who
justifies? Who is he who condemns?" (Romans
8:31-34).

So there is a multitude of ways the New Testament makes clear that we need rescue, and the rescue is real. It isn't just about getting snatched away
from someone who has kidnapped you. It is a lifetime of being joined to the family of God and to
God himself.

There is a lifetime of dynamic interactions with
God here. But we must believe we need the rescue.

We need to let God pull us away from our captivity so that the confusion in our minds can clear up. And then one of the most precious words in our vocabulary will be saved.

PRAY THIS
Lord, I know that sometimes I try to tell myself that I really don't need to be rescued. And I realize how foolish that is. It is easier for me to ignore my real spiritual needs than to face them. But in your saving arms are kindness, grace, and mercy. You have done what I cannot do for myself. So please help me to loosen my grip on my own life and to experience your daily saving work in my life.

KNOWING HIM

ESSAY

CROSS AND TOMB

Excerpt (chapter 13) from *Putting the Pieces Back Together: How Real Life and Real Faith Connect* by Mel Lawrenz (Zondervan, 2005)

"He who knows the mystery of the cross and tomb, also knows the essential principles of all things."

—Maximus Confessor

I was walking through the tiled corridor of the history building at the University of Wisconsin, having just finished teaching a class, my mind focused on pressing ahead to the cafeteria for a bite to eat. But my way was blocked by a cluster of twenty or so students who stood motionless and quiet, staring up at a TV monitor mounted high on a wall in the lobby, listening to the news anchor's low and slow voice, which echoed among the tile and stone. I too could only stop and look up.

There on the monitor was a picture of a few dozen people in an outdoor reviewing stand-and they too were looking up, straining to see something, heads tilting, hands shielding their eyes from the sun. The next shot was of a strange pillar of smoke that branched out in two directions at the top. I heard a student whisper to another who just joined the cluster, "The Challenger blew up. The space shuttle." And the other student said in a hushed whisper, "No way."

Though I may not remember what I did or where I was the day before yesterday, I remember exactly where I was standing when I heard that the space shuttle blew up just after launch, though that was seventeen years ago now. We all looked up, and have looked up a hundred times since seeing video replays of that yellow and black explosion, the chaos in the sky, the cross-like shape of the smoke with a fireball at the middle. We can only imagine what happened at that moment when seven brave explorers became martyrs in their cause.

Christ Lifted Up

"When I am lifted up from the earth, I will draw all people to myself." Of all Jesus' statements pointing to his cross and what would happen in the world because of his crucifixion, this is one of the most poignant. He said this, according to John, "to indicate the kind of death he was going to die." Flesh nailed to a cross piece, hoisted up on a post, hanging in such a way that it was hard to draw a breath. Left to dry, left to die. And all that the people around could do was to stop, and look up. But as they looked up at the torture, they were also looking up toward heaven, and the world-changing transaction that was taking place at this crossing point.

There were the crowds who flowed out of Jerusalem, following the procession out to the "Place of the Skull" as we might follow an ambulance to a smoking heap beside the road. Gapers' block. Hard not to look, hard not to slow down.

"The people stood watching..." (Luke 23:35).

Jesus' own followers followed him to that place that they did not want to go to. "A large number of people followed him, including women who mourned and wailed for him" (Luke 23:27). They dared not stand too close. "But all those who knew him, including the women who had followed him from Galilee, stood at a distance, watching these things" (Luke 23:49).

Some of those close by participated in the crime, soldiers for whom a crucifixion was one more dirty duty on one more dirty day in the desert so far away from home. "The soldiers also came up and mocked him. They offered him wine vinegar and said, 'If you are the king of the Jews, save yourself'" (Luke 35:36-37).

The authorities who saw the wooden post as a decisive way to lance the boil of Jesus' ministry, to be rid of the problem once and for all, "sneered at him. They said, 'He saved others; let him save him-

self is he is the Christ of God, the Chosen One'"
(Luke 35:35).

We all seek salvation. People use different
words for it, but really all people living in all places
at all times recognize through injury and disap-
pointment and death that something has gone ter-
ribly wrong in the world, and we need rescue.

So when the soldiers ridiculed Jesus by saying
that he should save himself from his torture, and
when the rulers claimed that the least the "Messiah"
should be able to do is to save himself, and when
one of the criminals being crucified next to Jesus
taunted, "Aren't you the Christ? Save yourself and
us," they all spoke through bitter, teeth-clenched
mouths of their own most deep personal need to be
saved-but in a way they could barely imagine.

They all looked up. How could they not?

When Jesus was lifted up in that way at that
time, he did draw all people to himself. In his book,
The Cruciality of the Cross, P. T. Forsyth wrote,
"Christ is to us just what his cross is. All that Christ
was in heaven or on earth was put into what he did
there...Christ, I repeat, is to us just what his cross is.
You do not understand Christ til you understand
his cross."

What did Jesus want us to understand about his cross? And why did he "endure the cross, scorning its shame" because of the "joy set before him" (Hebrews 12:2)? It was because Jesus knew that when he would be "lifted up" he would draw all people to himself.

It is an insult and a source of anguish for Jesus that the human race is broken in so many ways-scattered, disrupted, and alienated. Left in pieces. Something was needed to draw people together, reconciled first to God and then to each other. When Jesus was lifted up, when his friends and followers stood stunned, and when even his bitterest enemies focused on his waning life, then he became the focal point of all human vision. And we have not been able to look away from the cross since. Think of all the places you see crosses today, and consider that even though we do not cringe at its horror when we glance at it up high on a church steeple or dangling loosely on a gold chain around a woman's neck, we still choose to focus on it. How can we not?

The crossroad of Golgotha was a great gathering of a scattered humanity. Some walked away no less scattered than before. But a marker had been planted on a hill that would keep us piecemeal people looking toward him and what he did that was utterly different from what any martyr had ever done. Was he a mock "king of the Jews," as the insulting sign placed above his head said? A Messiah who could not save himself? Or could he truly respond to that dying criminal's request, "Jesus, remember me when you come in your kingdom," with "Today, you will be with me in paradise"?

It's hard for us to know how that criminal who died next to Jesus could have had faith in Jesus on that day when Romans soldiers ripped and bloodied him, but he did. He didn't have the advantage that we do of seeing Jesus in his death and in his resurrection.

Treasure Out of Tombs

Howard Carter and a few workmen made their way down an ancient 30-foot passageway cut into the rock in the Valley of the Kings in Egypt. For over 3,000 years, no human had stepped down that corridor. At the end, Carter began cutting a hole in the door until he peered inside and saw "wonderful things."

He was a sickly and lonely boy in England in the late 1800's, but a visit to an Egyptian exhibit in London sparked young Howard's imagination. As a young man he became an artist, and landed a job as a tracer with the Egyptian Exploration Fund. He joined Sir Flinders Petrie on an archaeological dig in Egypt and began learning Arabic and the science of digging. In 1900 he was given permission to begin his own dig and for years he scratched around in the rock and dirt.

Breaking into the chamber, Carter was astonished to be standing among elaborate vases, couches, statues, jewelry, chariots, and a beautiful ostrich feather fan that stood in perfect condition. The scent of perfume still hung in the air. But then in another chamber came the big surprise, a solid gold coffin containing the mummified remains of King Tutankhamen, a solid gold mask covered the face, and a wreath of flowers on top of it. No one had ever seen a spectacularly rich tomb of an Egyptian king that had gone undiscovered and undisturbed by robbers. And it was all sealed up in the general era of the great Exodus of the Israelites-one of the greatest moments of salvation the world had ever seen.

Tombs are sometimes places of epiphany, but
none more so than the one used for Jesus. His tomb
was sealed in Jerusalem about 1400 years after
young King Tut's. His was the burial of one judged
a criminal, and mocked as a make-believe king.
Those who loved Jesus dignified his burial with
love and care. His tomb, however, did not remain
undisturbed. It was cracked open within days of
the burial, but not by human hands. And when first
a few women, then a few men entered they found...
absolutely nothing. Grave cloths lay empty and
useless. There were no statues or vases or piles of
jewelry. No gold. No regal accessories. This tomb
was not fit for a king, and it certainly was not fit for
the King of Kings, who had no intention of linger-
ing under the false pretense of perfumes.

And yet in that emptiness were riches none of
us can comprehend even now. The power of God-
by which Jesus came to life in the tomb, left the
tomb, and left the earth in a confident rebuke of all
of our greatest enemies, including death-has been
unleashed in the world.

Now, any of us can choose whether to hope that
we have enough gold in the tomb to make ourselves comfortable in the coffin, or whether we

have the vivifying Spirit of Christ filling the decayed parts of our lives now, and carrying us along with the promise of eternal life.

Look at this phrase: "the unsearchable riches of Christ." The apostle Paul uses an adjective here (Ephesians 3:8), "unsearchable," which means something so great you can't track or trace it. You can't really get your mind around it. It is unsearchable, untraceable, unfathomable, inexhaustible, inscrutable, incalculable, infinite. No matter how much gold you put in a tomb or in a bank account, there is always limit to its measure.

But the riches of Christ go beyond all measurement. There is no scale in the realm of human experience that can quantify it. Human love is only a hint of the love of God. Acts of mercy we read about in the newspaper are just a trickle compared to the flow of mercy that comes from God. Forgiveness is something that is so satisfying when we break open our clutches on someone else and are freed from resentment, but that is just a faint shadow of the forgiveness that God offers us in Christ.

In Ephesians 2 Paul also talks about riches:

But because of his great love for us, God, who is rich in mercy, made us alive with Christ even when we were dead in our transgressions-it is by grace you have been saved. And God raised us up with Christ and seated us with him in the heavenly realms in Christ Jesus, in order that in the coming ages he might show the incomparable riches of his grace, expressed in his kindness to us in Christ Jesus.

Here's the real promise: if you want to know treasure in life, then realize that it comes from being treasured by God.

I had a few thousand people participate in a survey about a year ago, and I asked a simple question: If you could ask God one thing, what would it be? Some of the most frequent answers did not surprise me, but this one caught my attention: many people wanted to ask God, why-why, O God-do you bother to love human beings? Frankly, I was startled that so many people asked that question.

For all the people that presume God's grace ("What else, after all, would God do?" they think. "Isn't love his full-time job?"), there are multitudes that wonder, "Why would God love them? Why would God love me?"

I don't know how you answer that, except to say (as the Bible does), that he just does. Surely the fact that there is no separate reason, no external necessity why God loves other than that he chooses to, makes it all the richer and more certain.

Cross and tomb go together in the Christian gospel: both were occupied for a short span, both abandoned, both defeated. The apostle Paul, who knew what it was to suffer for choosing to be associated with Jesus, said, "I want to know Christ and the power of his resurrection and the fellowship of sharing in his sufferings, becoming like him in his death" (Phil. 3:10). Paul wrote this at a time when he was in prison and anticipated that he would have his final trial and execution at any time. What helped him hold things together, and hold the meaning of it all together, is that when we are torn to pieces by enemies, we are known and can know the Lord who is also crushed by his enemies. But on the other side of the apparent defeat is the victory of resurrection.

This applies not just to apostles or to Christians about to be martyred, but to every believer who feels that life gets too shredded. Evil seems stronger than it should. Things in life are just getting broken up.

There is no greater promise that God can put the pieces of our lives back together than the resurrection of Jesus. We all know that at the moment of death, a body begins to break down. But Jesus' body did not go through that corruption. The resurrection of Jesus is the greatest miracle, not because it was so difficult. (Isn't the creation of the universe a larger physical feat? Isn't the conception of human life from two single seeds from mother and father a more amazing biological event?) Jesus got up and walked out of his tomb more easily than I got out of bed this morning.

No, the resurrection of Jesus is the greatest miracle because it signifies the greatest truth. The law of entropy, of things coming to pieces, is switched off in the resurrection of Jesus. He would not become dust, and so he proclaimed to us dust creatures that our lives do not need to fall to pieces. The power by which Jesus was raised from the dead brings marriages together, holds us together despite our diverse roles in life, and stops sin from taking us apart like a vicious virus attacking a body.

The Christian gospel says, consider the cross and take courage from the empty tomb. Cross and tomb work together. One is incomplete without the other. If Jesus had only died a martyr for a cause, but not been resurrected, then we might gain inspiration, but not salvation. If Jesus had been brought back to life, but after having died of natural causes, he would only be an example of miraculous resuscitation, not transformation. But he died a death of salvation, and rose from the dead in a transfigured body.

Cross and tomb are twin beacon lights.

Beacons of Salvation

Over the years, I have been interested in lighthouses, probably because Door County, Wisconsin, where I grew up, has many lighthouses around its 200-mile shoreline. There are treacherous shoals around this peninsula, and in the days of wooden ships, hundreds were lost. A great, great uncle of mine lost his ship on one of the shoals, and I've gone scuba-diving on many of the wrecks.

My greatgrandfather was the lighthouse keeper at Cana Island lighthouse, where treacherous autumn Lake Michigan storms beat against it, and my grandmother lived as a child in the lighthouse. I have always seen lighthouses as a vivid symbol of salvation, because I imagine myself in a wooden sailing ship, out in the violent waves of a November Lake Michigan storm, heaving a sigh of relief upon sighting a lighthouse, and knowing exactly where I am.

In a place called Bailey's Harbor, about halfway up the peninsula, there is a different kind of lighthouse. At the shore is a small white clapboard tower with a light in the top, just 20 feet or so off the ground. And then, set back from the shore about 200 yards is the main lighthouse. The trees are all cleared in that stretch between the two lights so that a boat off the shore can see both lights. The idea of this arrangement, called a range light, is that the captain of a boat can find not just a lighthouse, but, when he lines up those two lights, his precise location-and a safe way through the shoals.

The death and resurrection of Jesus are two beacons; one is incomplete without the other. But line them both up and you understand exactly what the purpose of Christ's death is and the power of his resurrection. Saving sacrifice works with triumphant resurrection. God is at work on the cross and in the tomb to our benefit.

And so you know exactly where you are.

PRAY THIS

Dear God, I trust you when you say that you love me for no other reason than that it is what you choose. Thank you for loving me in the priceless sacrifice of Jesus. And thank you for loving me by breaking the bonds of death and giving me hope for the future.

KNOWING HIM

Do you ever wish you understood the Bible better?

Almost everyone does. Mature believers and new believers. Young and old. Those who have read the Bible for years and those just starting out.

How to Understand the Bible: A Simple Guide, will help you gain an overall perspective on the flow and meaning of Scripture. It addresses questions like: What is the big picture of the Bible? What about Bible translations? How should we understand the stories of the Old Testament? How should we interpret what the prophets had to say? How should we understand the teachings of Jesus? What was Jesus teaching in the parables? How can we hear God's voice in Scripture? What are the proper ways to apply Scripture to life tod

WORDWAY
WWW.WORDWAY.ORG

Made in the USA
San Bernardino, CA
04 March 2015